Flute Solos

Easy-to-intermediate arrangements designed to bring out the best qualities of the flute. The wide range of compositions include works by Beethoven, Brahms, Dvorak, Schubert and many others as well as folk songs, dances jigs and reels from all over the world.

Order No. AM 40197
US International Standard Book Number: 0.8256.2038.4
UK International Standard Book Number: 0.7119.0317.4

Exclusive Distributors:
Music Sales Corporation
257 Park Avenue South, New York, NY 10010, USA
Music Sales Limited
8/9 Frith Street, London W1V 5TZ, England
Music Sales Pty. Limited
120 Rothschild Street, Rosebery, Sydney, NSW 2018, Australia

Printed in the United States of America by
Vicks Lithograph and Printing Corporation

Amsco Publications
New York/London/Sydney

EVERYBODY'S FAVORITE
FLUTE SOLOS

CONTENTS

EVERYBODY'S FAVORITE
FLUTE SOLOS

CONTENTS BY COMPOSERS

Dancing Doll
(POUPEE VALSANTE)

ED. POLDINI

La Cinquantaine

GABRIEL MARIE

Flight of the Bumble-Bee

N. RIMSKY-KORSAKOFF

Le Cygne
(The Swan)

C. SAINT - SAENS

Rêverie

CLAUDE DE BUSSY

Two Guitars

Russian Gypsy Folk Song

Andante con moto

Chinese Dance
From the "Nutcracker Suite"

P. TSCHAIKOWSKY, Op. 71

Habanera
from "Carmen"

G. BIZET

Cradle Song

BRAHMS

Londonderry Air

Irish Folk Song

Gavotte

F. J. GOSSEC

Ave Maria

F. SCHUBERT

Molto Adagio e religioso

On Wings of Song

MENDELSSOHN

Souvenir

FRANZ DRDLA

June
(BARCAROLLE)

P. TSCHAIKOWSKY, Op. 37, No. 6

Spanish Dance

M. MOSZKOWSKI, Op. 12, No. 1

Nocturne

F. CHOPIN, Op. 9, No. 2

Then You'll Remember Me
(Bohemian Girl)

BALFE

Serenade

JOSEPH HAYDN

Andante cantabile

None But the Lonely Heart

TSCHAIKOWSKY

I Dreamt That I Dwelt In Marble Halls
(BOHEMIAN GIRL)

BALFE

Barcarolle
from "Tales of Hoffmann"

OFFENBACH

Sérénade

G. PIERNÉ

Scherzando
leggiero

Minuet in G

L. VAN BEETHOVEN

TRIO

Minuet D.C.

Minuet D.C.

La Donna è mobile
from "Rigoletto"

VERDI

Intermezzo sinfonico
(from Cavalleria Rusticana)

P. MASCAGNI

Ah! So Pure
(MARTHA)

VON FLOTOW

Minute Waltz

FR. CHOPIN, Op. 64, No. 1

Polonaise
From "Mignon"

THOMAS

Melody in F

ANTON RUBINSTEIN

Spring Song

(Songs without Words, No. 30)

F. MENDELSSOHN

Chanson Triste

TSCHAIKOWSKY, Op. 40, No. 2

Waltz

BRAHMS

Orientale
(THE KALEIDOSCOPE)

CESAR CUI, Op. 50

La Paloma

YRADIER

Humoreske

ANTON DVOŘÀK, Op. 101, No. 7

Serenade
(LES MILLIONS D'ARLEQUIN)

R. DRIGO

Song of India
(from the Legend Sadko)

N. RIMSKY-KORSAKOFF

Solvejg's Song

GRIEG

Berceuse
(From "JOCELYN")

B. GODARD

Andante

Andante
(cross left hand over right)

Annie Laurie

LADY SCOTT

The Last Rose of Summer

VON FLOTOW

Salut d'Amour
(LOVE'S GREETING)

E. ELGAR, Op. 12

Serenade

FRANZ DRDLA

Cradle Song

M. HAUSER, Op. 11

Irish Washerwoman
(JIG)

Arkansas Traveller
(COUNTRY DANCE)

Pop Goes the Weasel
(VIRGINIA REEL)

The Campbells are Coming
(SCOTCH DANCE)

Garry Owen
(IRISH JIG)

Paddy Whack
(IRISH JIG)

Money Musk
(REEL)

Kerry Dance
(IRISH JIG)

Sailor's Hornpipe

Fisher's Hornpipe